Benji's Day at the Fair

Nancy Stine

Illustrations by Polina Ipatova

First Printing, 2014

Printed in the United States of America

About the Author

Nancy Stine calls Michigan home although she has lived in the Florida Keys, the mountains of North Carolina, Las Vegas - and Northern Michigan. She treasures camping and times shared with her family. She loves spending time with her grandchildren and 2 great grandchildren. These Benji and Poppy stories developed as she watched the close and loving relationship between her son and his first grandchild.

DEDICATION

I wish to dedicate this book to all those loving grandparents and to their beautiful grandchildren.

~

May your relationships grow as your grandchildren grow to a productive and mature adulthood.

INTRODUCTION TO THE BENJI AND POPPY STORIES

In this time when both parents need to work to make ends meet, grandparents are often there to fill in the gaps - to provide experiences - to teach values.

Benji has a special loving relationship with his Poppy and Mimi. They spend quality time with him. They take him to the park or out for an ice cream cone. They read to Benji. They talk to him. They provide new experiences for him in order to develop his curiosity.

Today's adventure is a visit to the county fair as seen through the eyes of a 3 year old - in rhyme.

Poppy and I had a day at the fair.

The weather was fine. There was no rain there.

I was not sure of what I would see,

But when we arrived, I was so happy.

There were balloons, and clowns, and animals galore,

There were ponies to ride which I adore.

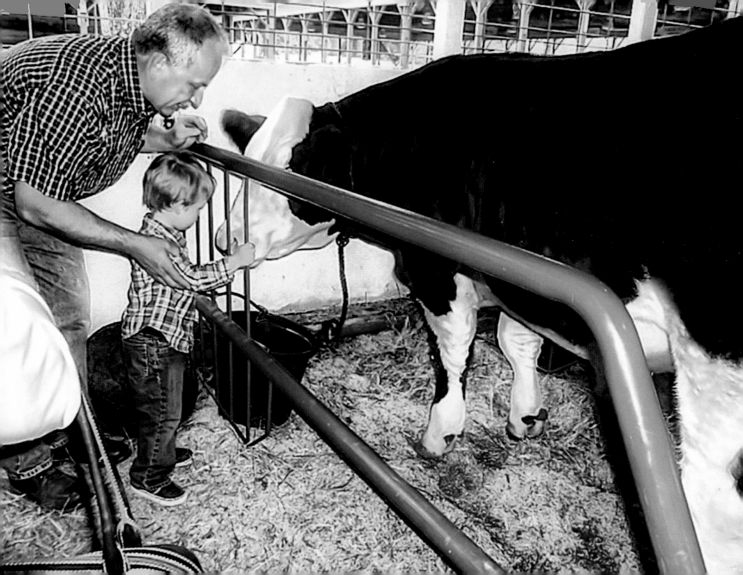

There was cotton candy, and corn on the cob.

A man making pizza. He sure liked his job.

The apples with caramel were all freshly made,

And I shared with my Poppy some cold lemonade.

We ate hot dogs and peanuts and dogs on a stick,

I ate way too much. I HOPE I'm not sick.

The next thing I saw were the animal barns,

I bee lined my way to see a goat with horns.

Lying beside her were two small bucks,

I reached in to touch them but had no luck.

The nanny goat butted my hand away.

She let out a noise as if to say.

Hey, these are my kids, so please use care.

Be gentle with them. They're new to the fair.

My Poppy, he laughed at that old nanny goat

And said, "You won't mind if I feed you some oats."

So he put some change into the coin slot.

And out came some oats, a cupful we got.

Then Poppy showed how to keep my hand flat

And nanny goat ate all my oats just like that.

The next pen we came to, there was a fat pig

She was clean as a whistle and oh, so big.

Under her belly, quite hidden from view

There were nine baby piglets, Oh my! That's quite a few!

And, can you believe it? Their tails are curly,

Their noses are wrinkled. Their skin is so pearly.

Those piglets, they rooted around with a squeal.

And I said, "Oh, Poppy, I've just got to feel.

Their skin looks so rough. Oh please let me in

to tickle some piglets under their chin."

Poppy said, "Benji, just reach in your hand

And give them a scratch, the best that you can."

Music was playing - and the merry-go-round

Was swirling and drawing me there with its sound.

Poppy bought tickets so we climbed aboard.

He lifted me up on the horse I adored.

It glittered – and galloped with me on its back

While sulkies were racing around on the track.

We went for a ride on an elephant's back.

I felt so scared, I thought I might yak.

My stomach flipped over as we went around.

And I was never so high, above the ground.

The people looked like ants, from the seat where I sat.

And it made me just wonder if birds thought like that.

The ponies were waiting and ready to go

Around the corral like an old rodeo.

I climbed on the gray one, all saddled and bound,

Holding on tight as we went around.

This was more fun than my merry-go-horse

The pony I'm riding is REAL, of course.

Poppy said, "Benji, you ride like a pro.

You look like a cowboy in a big rodeo."

I grinned when my horse made a whinny and blew

As if he were answering, "Oh boy, you sure do."

I wanted to stay there and ride him all day.

But Poppy said, "Time now to give him some hay."

"Your pony needs rest now, and Grandson, me too.

I think we should head home, Benji. Don't you?

Mimi is waiting and she'll want to hear

About the adventures you had at the fair.

Let's buy a nice treat to take home to her.

A big candy apple to show her we care."

I waved to the ponies as we walked away.

This surely has been my most favorite day.

I dreamed all the way home of what I would tell.

About all the rides, the fun and good smells.

And I would have given my Mimi her treat

If I had not fallen asleep in my seat.

It is very important for me to hear what you think about this book. Please leave me a review.

Thank you.

OTHER BOOKS BY Nancy Stine

Benji's Day at the Farm

Heal Yourself Naturally: with Clay

Heal Yourself Naturally: with Turmeric

BOOKS BY Kate Townsend O'Keefe

Kitza and Petey: Ghost Sensitives - The Wailing Ghost

Kitza and Petey: Ghost Sensitives - The Ghost With a Mission

Kitza and Petey: Ghost Sensitives - Justice

Clockwork Guardians

Blueprint

Made in the USA
Middletown, DE
05 June 2022